Supernatural Search
IN CORNWALL

MICHAEL WILLIAMS

BOSSINEY BOOKS

ACKNOWLEDGMENTS

Cover photography: RAY BISHOP

Other photographs: RAY BISHOP,; JOHN LYNE

Drawings: FELICITY YOUNG

First published in 1991 by Bossiney Books, St Teath, Bodmin, Cornwall.
Typeset and printed by Penwell Ltd, Callington, Cornwall.

ISBN 0 948158 68 9

ABOUT THE AUTHOR

– and the book

*M*ICHAEL WILLIAMS, a Cornishman, started full-time publishing in 1975. He and his wife Sonia live in a cottage on the shoulder of a green valley just outside St Teath in North Cornwall.

In addition to publishing and writing, Michael Williams is a keen cricketer and collector of cricket books and autographs. He was the first captain of the Cornish Crusaders Cricket Club and is today President of the Crusaders. He is also a member of Cornwall and Gloucestershire County Cricket Clubs. A member of the RSPCA and the International League for the Protection of Horses, he has worked hard for reform in laws relating to animal welfare. In 1984 he was elected to The Ghost Club, and is convinced Cornwall is the most haunted area in the whole of Great Britain.

Michael Williams is the author of Bossiney publications such as *Paranormal in the Westcountry, Supernatural in Cornwall* and *Superstition & Folklore*. He is currently collaborating with Polly Lloyd of Bristol on *Somerset Mysteries* and, as a publisher, he is now operating in six areas: Cornwall, Devon, Dorset, Somerset, Avon and Wiltshire.

Here, in his latest book *Supernatural Search in Cornwall*, he investigates a whole range of paranormal subjects: ghosts and Supernatural smells, haunted locations, and such questions as: 'Is there life after death for animals?'

UNFATHOMABLE CORNWALL …Author Michael Williams at the Hurlers. 'Cornwall is the most haunted area in the whole of Great Britain.'

GHOSTLY FOOTSTEPS … What spirit paces this corridor at Jamaica Inn, Bolventor?

SUPERNATURAL SEARCH IN CORNWALL

CORNWALL and the Supernatural relate naturally – like strawberries and Cornish cream.

The Cornish landscape has a haunted, haunting quality. There is scarcely a hamlet without a ghost.

Why?

As someone who has been investigating the Supernatural for more than a quarter of a century, I ought to know the answer – but I do not.

Maybe it is a combination of factors. Cornwall is a Celtic land; consequently we Cornish may be more attuned to psychic matters than most. In places too there is a timeless air – the difference between past and present very thin.

Of course, a percentage of alleged hauntings in Cornwall or anywhere else in the world can be explained and have nothing to do with the Supernatural. Psychosomatic disorders and hallucination could remove a fair number of so-called 'hauntings'. Others have a very natural explanation: a trick of light, or shadow, unexpected movement through a gust of wind, mistaken identity in the dark are only four areas for possible human error. But even if we dismiss fifty per cent of ghosts for one reason or another, the remaining fifty per cent represents a very solid body of evidence. The evidence for ghosts is so overwhelming that the only real debate centres on the nature of ghosts. Sightings have been too numerous, the descriptions often crystal-clear, in vivid detail, and sometimes the sightings have been a shared experience – as was my first case at Bossiney in 1965 which is reported in detail in *Supernatural in Cornwall*.

I have now interviewed more than 300 people claiming

Supernatural experience. Only a handful were crackpots. The great majority gave the impression of thoroughly reliable character. In many cases I have been struck by the matter of fact tone and come away with this impression: if these people have invented their experience, then they would have invented something more dramatic.

Typical was a recent account from Margaret Rowe of The Strand Bookshop at Padstow: 'It was late in August 1990 and only a few minutes from closing time. We keep open until ten o'clock in the season, and this lady came in. She was wearing a white top and black skirt – very modern type of dress – and she went to the back of the shop to look at some books, out of our view. When ten o'clock came, the three of us here thought it was time to close. We'd had a long day, but when we went to tell the lady it was closing time, she simply wasn't there. We even went upstairs to check that she might have wandered off up there. But no sign of her anywhere. All I can tell you is she came into the shop, but she didn't go out!'

Down on the other coast of Cornwall I had two conversations about a curious happening experienced by Donald Holder and his wife Sheila. They were driving back late one evening from Bodmin to Fowey with Donald at the driving wheel. Just before Fowey Cross, Donald braked violently to avoid a figure on the road: on the right, coming from Fowey. But there was no accident as the figure had just vanished. Donald assured me he had seen only one ghostly figure – gender uncertain – and Sheila assured me she had seen only one figure: that of a woman on the left hand side of the car!

There are, of course, various ghosts. Some are anniversary ghosts, in that they appear on a certain day or night. Others manifest themselves in certain kinds of weather. Some seem to relate to a very specific area; others tend to move about: the same ghost but seen in different locations.

Then there are unseen ghosts – a presence felt rather than a form seen. In 1989 I did a television programme with David Young for Television South West on hauntings at Jamaica Inn, Bolventor on Bodmin Moor. The inn has a haunted reputation, and I was interested to talk with Reginald Carthew who had worked at Jamaica Inn for more than fifty years. Bearded Reginald told me though he

THE LANDSCAPE … The timeless elements of cliffs and sea near Gurnard's Head captured here by artist Felicity Young.

had never seen a ghost at the inn, he had on many occasions 'been conscious of someone watching me. Then I'd look round and there'd be nobody there, but I was quite sure somebody had been watching me.'

Over the years a growing number of incidents at Bolventor have defied reasonable logical explanation: unexplained footsteps, the ghostly figure of a rider on horseback outside the inn, strange hoof-beats on the road and a ghost in a three-cornered hat in one of the bedrooms who finally disappeared through a large solid wardrobe. Earlier in the century too there was a stranger who stood drinking in the bar. He was called outside, but never returned to finish his drink. They found his murdered body next morning out on the moor. In the wake of that crime there was a volume of correspondence in *Country Life*: people claiming to see a strange man sitting on the wall outside the inn. Descriptions matched that of the murdered customer – and the general view was that the man sitting on the wall was, in fact, his ghost.

It is the down-to-earth type of account that impresses.

Our principal Bossiney photographer Ray Bishop, for instance, conversed with a dead man in a Wadebridge shop – and they talked about the weather! Ray also has in his possession the photograph of what he believes to be a ghost. Alas, we cannot publish the strange figure by a font in a Cornish Church: Ray, a man of his word, promised he would not do so years ago. But I have seen that picture – and am convinced it *is* a ghost.

Ray, of course, is not alone in possessing a 'spirit' photograph. Perhaps the most incredible example of spirit photography relates to Air Marshal Sir Victor Goddard. In this case the face of a dead airman appeared clearly in the back row of a group of service men. It was recognised as that of an airman who recently had tragically died by accidentally walking into the moving propellers of a plane. A copy of the extraordinary picture, taken immediately after this group had returned from the man's funeral service, lay on the Air

IN THE PICTURE … Michael Williams and his wife Sonia, photographer Ray Bishop and Bossiney author Sarah Foot celebrate Ray's 1,000th photograph for Bossiney.

CREATIVE SPIRIT ... Bossiney book illustrator and author Felicity Young tunes into a Barbara Hepworth sculpture at St Ives on a brilliant November morning.

Marshal's desk when he was writing his book *Flight Towards Reality* twenty years ago. You can see a very clear copy of this photograph in Brian Inglis's excellent book *The Paranormal, an Encyclopedia of Psychic Phenomena* published by Granada. I recommend it to all serious students of the Supernatural.

Then there are many people who though having Supernatural experience refuse to reveal those experiences for fear of ridicule.

One Cornish resident happily without such inhibition is Leila Ball. Writing from her home at Frogpool near Truro in August 1990, she recalled two experiences.

'One evening some twenty years ago during a spell of unemployment I decided to sort through some old letters and receipts of my mother's and her parents to while away a rather boring evening. I quickly glanced through several and tore them up. Soon there was quite a pile on the floor beside me. Suddenly the closed door leading into the dining room where I was sitting began to vibrate violently. It seemed as if two or three people were frantically trying to open the door. The handle was turned several times, and the panels were almost bending due to the force of blows. After some seconds I jumped to my feet expecting to see my uninvited guests but nobody came through the door. After perhaps ten or fifteen seconds (it seemed like hours) the noise stopped. I glanced at myself in the mirror and found myself as white as a ghost. I remember thinking to myself "I wonder what caused that." It must have been something to do with the remains of the letters I had torn up. I quickly gathered the others up and put them away again, and never touched them until two years ago when I sorted them out and put them in the old box my mother used to keep them in.

'My second visit from my unusual guests caught me by surprise. It was rather an amusing encounter. I had moved flats and was now living two streets away from my old flat. I was sitting in the lounge and got up to get something from the other side of the room. As I walked towards the old oak sideboard I remember thinking that I had better throw away the fading pink rose that was in a vase on the sideboard, before the petals dropped off. To my delight the rose moved slowly from side to side three or four times almost as if to say – there, not a petal fell! I kept the rose and placed it in a glass jar where it is to this day. Another ten years has passed, and I am hoping for another visit from my ghost.'

The landscape of Cornwall can work on us in a variety of ways. For example, I cannot walk across the bleached grasses of Penwith moorland or Bodmin Moor, and not feel related to earlier events. Some of us live in the past as well as the present, and it is in these remoter moorland regions that this realization is often strongest.

Some years ago the author Denys Val Baker related an interesting story, when dining with us at Bossiney. He used the cottage of a friend in Penwith as the setting for a story. 'I attempted to capture the elemental side of life in Cornwall,' Denys explained. He was very attracted to the hills and the moorland, and in his story he coupled the landscape to the Bohemian lifestyle of artists and writers, bringing the tale to a climax with a mock observation of ancient Druidic sacrifices, 'In my story there was a death and I was shaken to find out later that in real life there was a similar case of someone going to spend a night there only to be found dead next morning!' Denys called it 'a sort of pre-vision.'

Denys Val Baker was one of a formidable army of writers who have come to Cornwall and found inspiration here.

Why has more been written, painted and created here than anywhere else in Britain outside London?

The question is inevitable; the answer elusive. Maybe Denys himself got close to the matter when he reflected: 'It is a mixture of material and mystical, facts and fantasies, all equally important.' Does a Supernatural factor come into this matter of creativity?

Thackeray said in *Roundabout Papers*: 'I have been surprised at the observations made by some of my characters. It seems as if an occult power was moving my pen.' Keats once admitted that he had 'not been aware of the beauty of some thought or expression' until after he had written it down on paper. It were as if the words 'had been written by someone else . . .' And the great Blake discussing his poem *Milton* stated: 'I have written this poem from immediate dictation, twelve or sometimes twenty or thirty lines at a time, without premeditation, and even against my will.'

Messages from out there?

More than twenty years ago I interviewed an elderly lady at Bude who claimed she was 'an automatic writer', that she merely relayed the messages, insisting the vocabulary and the sentiments expressed on the page had nothing to do with her.

In the early days of my Supernatural investigations I had reservations and declined to include some of her examples in my book *Supernatural in Cornwall*. Now it is too late. I no longer have her notes and she is dead – and am inclined to think it was me – not her – who was at fault. After twenty five years of investigation I now veer strongly to the view that limits exist only in our minds.

I have only been interested in white witches – those who operate for good purposes. A man who knows a great deal about many

14

TIMELESS TERRAIN ... High ground between St Ives and Zennor: 'The landscape of Cornwall can work on us in a variety of ways.'

forms of magic is Cecil Williamson who runs the witchcraft museum at Boscastle. He told me: 'The simple fact of life is that all magic making depends upon the help and participation of a spirit force. A force which, as a thought form is silent, and yet has the pulse of life. How to establish a union and understanding with this Supernatural force is the secret of your Cornish Aunty May. Why Aunty May? Well, with the true Celtic nimble wit of the Cornish, the answer is: "Maybe she will help you or maybe not!" So going to see Aunty Maybe got shortened to "Go and see Aunty May." '

In his publication *Westcountry Witches – What They Think and What They Do* Cecil Williamson mentions their night life style: 'She is never lonely, for she has as her constant and good companion her familiar spirit, her guardian angel. She values every passing minute of the day, and tries to get as much joy out of being alive as she is able. Her time is spent close to nature in the woods, fields and hills. Her companions are the trees, plants and animals. She is a loner and moves in lonely places, yet she is never alone. Unlike most people she is endowed with a Third Eye which once one has learnt to open and use same the world becomes an entirely different place. People have eyes and they see not, ears and they hear not. Witches are given to using the hours of darkness in which to move around. As any wild animal will tell you, the world is a far better place when the mass of human beings are out of sight tucked up in bed.'

The summit of Rough Tor on Bodmin Moor is one of the great grandstands of Cornwall. The rock formation is fantastic. It's a setting that stirs the imagination. You have these incredible stones: Daphne du Maurier wrote of them: 'Shaped like giant furniture with monstrous chairs and twisted tables.' Back in the 1960s I was doing a lot of journalism for a Cornish magazine, which had been founded by the great 'Q', and it was agreed that I would write a feature called 'On the Roof of Cornwall.' So early one September morning I set off with a photographer and a tan and white terrier called Tex. The higher we climbed the more apprehensive the little dog became, and that was strange because he was normally a pugnacious character. Once on top the photographer got to work with his camera, but Tex hid in a crevice. Brown Willy beyond had a wonderfully beckoning quality, but the dog refused to go another inch. I thought he was seriously ill. We called off the whole project. I picked him up and resolved to go straight to Camelford and visit Mr. Byrne the veterinary surgeon there. The dog's tremors were so violent that I thought he was going to die. Then halfway down the slope Tex started struggling. He scampered away a totally different dog. Did he detect something beyond our human vision that morning? I don't know and frankly I've never had such a frightening experience as that morning on Rough Tor in all my Supernatural investigations. It had no Supernatural context and yet there was something very disturbing about it.

Curiously, I have been on the summit many times since, and have never found it in the least sinister. But something that morning triggered this apprehension, this great fear. Years after that September experience the author James Turner told me how sentries of the old Volunteers encamped nearby had seen the ghost of Charlotte Diamond, a Cornish girl murdered by her jealous lover one Sunday in 1844.

Tom Lethbridge, the man they called the 'Einstein of the Paranormal,' lived for some years in Devon and made visits to Cornwall. Lethbridge believed that nature somehow generates 'fields of static electricity' in certain locations, especially those close to running water. These 'fields', he maintained, were able to record

GRANDSTAND OF CORNWALL ... Daphne de Maurier wrote: 'Shaped like giant furniture with monstrous chairs and twisted tables.'

the thoughts and responses of people. Consequently if we go into a place where a murder was committed years ago or where someone committed suicide, we may detect an unpleasant atmosphere. Yet all that is happening is the emotions, associated with the earlier murder or suicide, are being transferred to us – in accordance with the laws of electricity.

Likewise if we go to a place and are feeling happy and full of energy, then our feelings will be recorded on that field.

WESTERN MOORLAND ...Rocky tors with grass and heather slopes below and a clear Cornish sky above beckon those in quest of the elusive spirit of Cornwall.

18

ANIMALS AND THE SUPERNATURAL

G HOST sightings in Cornwall have been numerous. Ghost sounds less so, and as an animal lover I have long been interested in animal hauntings.

Ghostly hoof beats brought Rebecca Pickford of BBC Radio Cornwall and me to Ventongimps, a quiet valley near Perranporth. We came at the invitation of Jack Benney, a fellow Cornishman and keen student of the Supernatural.

On a balmy May afternoon, the three of us stood in a sloping green field.

'I was working in this meadow. It was a lovely afternoon in early summer; hardly a breath of air,' Jack recalled. 'I had been cultivating this piece of land with a rotavator and stopped to rest, when all of a sudden I became aware of the sound of a horse's hoof beats galloping along what is locally called the Church Road. The sound was very distinct. There are steep fields on both sides of the valley which I'm sure would produce a megaphone or amplifier of any sound in the valley below.

'I don't suppose I would have taken any notice if the sound of the hoof beats had continued until out of hearing. But all of a sudden the hoof beats stopped *abruptly* in the direction of the bridge or on it. There was no slowing down to a trot or a walk, but this sudden and complete silence.'

'What did you do then?' probed Rebecca.

'Well,' said Jack, 'I went down to the bottom hedge of this little meadow and from there I looked down on to the bridge, and there was no sign of an animal at all.'

'That must have bemused you.' Rebecca made it sound like half

HAUNTING HOOVES … The pony that gallops on at Ventongimps in endless pursuit of its long-dead rider.

JOURNEY'S END ... Jack Benney and Felicity Young on the bridge where the galloping hoofbeats abruptly stop.

a statement, half a question.

'Yes,' continued Jack. 'That's the very thing that made me stop and think. Perhaps in the past an accident happened at the bridge, involving a rider and horse. Maybe a horse or pony bolted along the Church Road and struck the stone wall of the bridge killing the rider. The terror, given off by both rider and horse, could have been absorbed by the immediate surroundings, which acted like a tape recorder, retaining the violent and tragic happening until a build up of atmosphere caused it to explode into a sighting or sound of what happened in that area perhaps years ago. Is there, I wonder, a fourth dimension out of our three dimensional world which at times of tragedy overlaps our seeing world for a brief moment? – until the energy built up over a certain period of time or anniversary of the happening exhausts itself, and then fades away from our sight until a future time or date.'

Jack Benney then recalled the experience of two local people. They had been out for the evening and were returning to Ventongimps, when in the headlights of their car, they saw a pony standing in the road.

'It was outside a field gate of a smallholding and they came from the Truro direction, and as they rounded the corner they saw in the headlights a pony standing in the road. Well, the pony started to trot down the road in front of them and they followed it a bit down the road, around the corner and over the little stone bridge that we mentioned a moment ago. They took it to be a real pony and they followed it to their residence. The pony went up over the little brow and when they got up near a field gate it stopped in the middle of the road. The lady got out of the car, went up to stroke the pony which she says she did, and then opened the gate to the little meadow to let it in, and as they turned around the pony faded in their vision. Just disappeared, into thin air, in front of their car.'

Our investigation now led us to another local resident Leonard Rice.

'I was over in the garden one evening and the horse came galloping down the road; it's not unusual for horses to come up and down here but not usual to hear one galloping down the road. Then it stopped. I thought that was funny, so I went down the bottom of the garden, looked out over the hedge, over to the bridge – nothing there.'

'So you were expecting to see a horse there and perhaps something had gone wrong?' asked Rebecca.

'That's right, nothing was there.'

'Had you heard Jack's account of this story when you heard these hoofbeats?'

'No I hadn't. When I heard, I went down to the farm in the

evening and I said to Mrs Hayes "A funny thing happened tonight: a horse came down the road, and when I looked there was nothing there." "Well," she said, "that's the ghost of Ventongimps," and her story was that the horse had run away, that it crashed into the bridge and there was a girl killed.'

An interesting postscript to our visit came in the form of a letter from Jack Benney. In it Jack wrote: 'What we both said and thought was borne out by Leonard Rice's later account of a horse and rider crashing into the bridge, killing the rider, a girl, according to the late

QUIET LANE … Retaining its mystery, even on a sunny day, the lane where the ghost horse has been seen.

Mrs Hayes.

'I hadn't heard that story before Leonard mentioned it in the radio interview. Wasn't it strange then that you and I had *separately* come to the belief that a horse had crashed into the bridge. There doesn't appear to be a set time for it to manifest either by sound or appearance. It must have been a very powerful recording on the immediate vicinity at the time of the accident. I heard it one afternoon in early summer; Leonard one evening, Patsy Weaver one night . . . and the couple who saw the pony late one evening past midnight. It (the pony) must have appeared very solid because the gentleman said it was "a roan colour." If it is the same that crashed into the bridge, then its wanderings cover the three approaches to the bridge, forming a trivium, where hauntings may occur according to Colin Wilson.'

Thanks to Jack Benney, I was soon back in the Perranporth area on another Supernatural search.

It was Jack who kindly made an appointment with two ladies, a Cornish housewife who prefers to remain anonymous, and her friend Kay Marshall who formerly lived in London.

'It was September,' the Cornish housewife recalled, 'and we decided to go for a walk to the lost church. As soon as St. Piran's Cross came into view my Yorkshire terrier started acting as if he had seen a giant or something – absolutely terrified. He's got this long hair and it absolutely lifted off his back. I'd never seen a dog with hair standing up like it in my life! We couldn't believe it.'

'What made you think it was the cross?'

'Because when we walked around the perimeter of the cross, he behaved in this very, very nervous manner; and we ourselves felt an evil presence. Funnily enough, we had another dog with us but he just kept sniffing the grass as dogs normally behave. The moment we turned to walk back to the cross, testing him, we again felt this presence.'

Kay continued the story: 'We went to the cross a second time with the dog, and he was just the same – just as if he was seeing someone with a stick – sort of dodging about as if he couldn't really believe his eyes and again he didn't want to go anywhere near the cross. We both felt it too; more so in fact. I don't say we fled, but we certainly hurried away. You had a feeling "Let's go!" and you had a job not to run.'

Her colleague then told me of a third expedition to St. Piran's Cross: 'This time I went with my brother and sister-in-law. Naturally I told them about the previous visits. The dog behaved not quite as badly on the earlier occasions, but there is obviously *something* there that disturbs him. He was very agitated. We went into the church area, and you felt it even in there that day. I don't think our minds are taking over. But my sister-in-law pointed out an arrangement of stones in a circle, the big one at the end – and we came to the conclusion it might be witchcraft.'

'This was out of character for the dog?'

'Oh yes, I tested him immediately after, we previously met people out walking as they do at the lost church, and he didn't take any notice, and afterwards I said perhaps someone came up to him quickly. When we saw someone we kept quiet, but no, he never misbehaved any more. Later I came across a very old book about the cross and how it was pagan and used for evil, and then the whole site had been Christianised.'

Jack Benney now came into the conversation:

'There is certainly an atmosphere up there; you don't feel it every time, but I've been up there a number of times. I went up in 1986 after the service that they hold there at 3pm the last Sunday in October, and all the people had wandered back across the sand dunes before I went up there from the oratory. I had a pendulum and I had a very strong reaction. I put my hand on the west facing side, the pendulum swung in a wide arc, in the clockwise direction, and when I went to the east side the pendulum went the opposite way round. Quite strong, and my dowsing rod that I made is very very sensitive; when I put that one on the west face, it swung around and struck that cross so hard it bounced back. Hamish Miller the professional dowser says there's a tremendous radiation aura around the stone. He says at least fifteen feet, he went right around the circle. He says there's an energy line running from the cross right over the Penhale point. He was quite impressed when he saw it!'

Kay Marshall then recalled another experience with the lost Church.

'You know how it's covered. Well, I have walked between the

ANCIENT MAGIC ... St Piran's Cross – a disturbing aura surrounds the cross which may be linked to pagan rituals.

walls, quite happily, and thought fancy me being able to do all this after all these years. But later on it got flooded, right up to the door, and I came upon it. I was looking for it coming down the dunes, as I saw that I drew back quickly because it frightened me to death, and it's only rainwater over the dent that I've walked through.

'It was a feeling that I should think you'd have if you were going to be swung, as I crawled back up the dunes, and went down there. It looked so horrible, and I've never felt that before. Just rainwater in the hollow up to the door, but it really terrified me. I've never really liked it since. It was something there that hadn't been there before, just when it was underwater. That water looked evil, and yet I knew it wasn't even deep, it was only just the hollow, just full of water. I felt as though I didn't dare stand up, I stepped back, lay back on the dunes, and went back on my elbows. I've never felt that I could possibly walk through those walls again.'

Later Jack Benney told me more about the cross: 'The cross is sited near and in line with the east end of the old parish church. There are schools of thought that the site may have been of pagan origin where the sacrifice of humans may have taken place. Great importance was attached to the human head by the early Celts, when heads were placed above and either side of the doorway of the places of pagan worship. Even in early Christian times in Celtic places of worship, heads of stone adorned the doorway, as were found at St. Piran's Oratory. It's interesting that when the oratory was excavated in 1835 by William Mitchell of Truro, three skeletons were discovered beneath the altar minus their heads which were found buried near the south door.'

Jack further clarified Kay Marshall's reference to 'the lost church'. 'She was,' explained Jack, 'talking about the site of the oratory before it was reburied under a mound of sand in October 1980. The area Kay described was the surrounding depression or area of the then remains of the oratory covered by that unsightly concrete structure and she said she had walked between the walls. She was talking about walking between the remaining walls of the oratory itself and the inner walls of the protecting concrete shell. Kay also

SECRET OF THE DUNES … St Piran's Oratory, deep in the sand.

mentioned the water which floods the site during the winter months or after a period of prolonged rain. There has always been water beneath the floor of the oratory or visible in it. I can remember going there in the 1920s, say about 1925-27, when you walked on duck boards or slatted lengths of wood to prevent getting wet feet. There is to the west of the oratory a spring, now many feet below the mounds of sand that surrounds the site.

'No wonder Kay felt afraid of walking through the water, little knowing that beneath lie hundreds of human remains, some dating back to the sixth century. It was the wish of the dying to be buried as close to the remains of the Saint as possible; so a great concentration of bodies lay around the oratory, which was proved to be the case, when in 1835 a great storm uncovered thousands of human bones, some entire, all facing east to west and bleached white by the sand and time.'

SEEING BEYOND … Tex the terrier, whose odd behaviour on the summit of Rough Tor was quite out of character.

30

LIFE AFTER DEATH – FOR ANIMALS?

A NIMAL ghosts invariably lead us to ask an important question. Is there life after death for the animal kingdom?

One woman who has no doubts is Marilyn Preston Evans of Saltash. A well known animal – and human – healer here in the Westcountry, she told me:

'Yes, I now firmly believe that animals still live on after what we term "death". In fact I know now that nothing and no-one can possibly die. We merely move out of our physical body, as do our animal and bird friends – this can be actually witnessed by clairvoyants at the time of transition of all life forms. Also many people, apart from clairvoyants, have seen animal "ghosts" – in fact it was through a spirit dog near Bude that I met my present husband. There are many stories I could tell of animal survival after so-called death. One of these is about Ben, an oldish cat who had been a stray and who was rescued by a very caring lady living near Looe in Cornwall. Ben was never a well cat and was nicknamed "the coconutmatcat" because his long browny fur grew in different directions; he was a most gentle and affectionate cat under the loving, tender care of Hazel and Derek, who had also given a home to three other cats at the time. But Ben became ill and was diagnosed by the vet as having leukaemia. He treated him for this and Ben was also brought to me for healing. He was 'up and down' for quite a long while, until finally one day Hazel telephoned in tears to say that Ben had died that morning.

We were both in tears. I ended by saying that perhaps Ben would be able to "come back" and tell them he was all right now. That same evening Derek called to his wife that Ben was sitting on the mantlepiece – laughing! They then realised he had been afraid of heights before, and was telling them he now wasn't. Some ten days after Ben's body was buried, Hazel went to take a photo of Morti, the large black short-haired cat, lying in a ray of sunshine in the lounge. However, she then found the film had run out in the camera and made a hasty change with a new film before Morti moved. She was then dumbfounded to see that Morti had suddenly become Ben! Talking firmly to herself, she said "Hazel – pull yourself together – Ben is dead." But she was still looking at Ben, stretched out in the sunshine. She took the photo and put the camera down, shaking. Looking again, she saw Morti.

'Hazel telephoned me to say what had happened, and was very shaken. I replied that perhaps it was indeed Ben who had returned to be photographed. Several months later, Hazel again telephoned. Could she come and see me with something? Arriving, she showed me the photographs she had just collected from being processed, together with one taken a year before of Ben lying down asleep, long, brownish fur going in different directions. One of the just-collected batch was of Morti, sitting up in his thick, black, short-fur coat. The other was of Ben lying half asleep in the sunshine of the lounge, with his claws extended in ecstasy, his browny-black 'coconutmatcat' long fur going in different directions! Ben had returned ten days after his "death" to be actually photographed by his grieving 'Mum!' One wonders what actually happened to Morti for the several moments Ben took over his space to be photographed. As I look at the photographs now in front of me I am still thrilled at this lovely happening that proves our animal friends do not die, any more than we do.

'Many people are naturally distressed to lose a pet – even though I now know they cannot die, it still distresses me, as we miss their physical presence so very much and unless we are gifted with clear-vision, we are then unable to see them in their changed frequency of light. I try to console many grieving people by explaining to them that the link of love, once forged between two beings, is *never* broken, and although the link cannot be seen, it is always there. When the natural time is right, they *will* meet again at a most joyous reunion – of that I have no doubt. When my loved ones pass on out of the physical garment they have worn for their earthly incar-

LINK OF LOVE … Marilyn Preston with an orphaned wild rabbit. She is convinced the link of love forged between two beings will always remain in this world and the next.

nation, I now always tell them, or rather ask them, to wait for me at home, in safety and I will see them there. My last words are usually "See you!" And I have a host of bird and animal friends at home waiting for me!

'Several years ago my first two dogs "died" tragically and I was deeply grieved. Although they had both been injected against distemper and hardpad and had booster injections, they both picked up the illness and suffered dreadfully for a long time while our vets did all possible to try to help them. In those days I had never heard of animal healing, of course, or the outcome might have been different. I became very depressed after their loss; previous to this I had lost my two baby boys prematurely and had no other family. At that time I had no idea that life was indeed continuous. A few weeks after Panda and Kim "died" the police sent another dog to us – a stray found in Plymouth. Lassie turned out to be a beautiful soul, too, and shortly after needed to be spayed. I was particularly worried about the operation, but a spirit doctor informed me I would be shown the evening before the operation that it would be all right. That evening I had an out-of-body experience and found myself in a lovely field of greener-than-green grass. Suddenly across the field came racing towards me my beloved Panda and Kim! I must say I have never seen them in all their years, looking so healthy and so happy! They were more alive than ever I had seen them on the earth plane, and we had a glorious game together, with me exclaiming "You're not dead!" It was almost unbelievable but I knew it was true and more real than when we were together before, in the physical body. I tried to pull some of Panda's wool out – she was/is an Old English Sheepdog – but she yelped and I couldn't get any to prove I had been with her, as I knew folk would not believe it when I told them. After that experience I never grieved for them again, because I know they are somewhere, just around the corner, waiting for me – at home in the real world!'

A ROYAL RESIDENCE

CORNWALL has the knack of springing surprises.

Tredethy Country Hotel at Helland Bridge is one such example.

Set in nine acres of trees and shrubs and overlooking one of the loveliest valleys in all Cornwall, Tredethy was once the home of royalty. When Prince Chula of Thailand was looking for a Westcountry home he chose wisely. The wooded sloping shoulders of the valley and the graceful movement of the River Camel on its way to join the Atlantic combine to give a magnificent view.

Before the Hitler war, Prince Chula owned and managed racing cars which were driven at great speeds by his cousin Prince Bira – they were well-known figures at Brooklands – but when peace returned Prince Chula Chakrabongse of Thailand (to give him his full title) devoted himself to writing, broadcasting, lecturing and making television appearances. He was a natural communicator and as an author he wrote on subjects as different as a life of Frederick the Great and a novel entitled *Three Daughters*. Naturally he wrote about motoring and racing and there was a splendid book called *First-Class Ticket, the Travels of a Prince*, which reflected his love of journeys.

I had the privilege of meeting the Prince on two occasions: at a Cornwall cricket match at Wadebridge and at the inaugural dinner of the Cornish Crusaders Cricket Club at the old Red Lion Hotel, Truro. That evening, he proposed the toast to the club and I had the difficult task of following him on the toast list – he was a very accomplished speaker, witty and wise.

I wonder how many visitors crossing the Tamar know of this royal

Thailand-Cornwall connection?

Today Tredethy is a delightful hotel offering comfort and a friendly atmosphere to visitors all through the calendar – in the winter months the log fires have a special warmth of their own.

But there is another side to Tredethy, a secret puzzling side. Tredethy has, in fact, something of a Supernatural reputation.

An old butler from long ago still moves about the place. He emerges from the former gun room and climbs the stairs, and he is clearly a ghost by virtue of the fact that he walks on a different level from the existing staircase. Considering the present staircase was built in 1868, we can safely assume he lived and worked here before that date.

Has he some connection with the ghostly lady who has been seen upstairs on the landing?

And why does Tra, the brown Burmese cat, spit at men on the staircase and sometimes behave aggressively on the stairs when she is seemingly alone? Cats, of course, are among the most psychic animals, and maybe she detects something beyond our limited human vision.

Cancerian Beryl Graham, who runs Tredethy with her husband Richard, says Tra never behaved like this in their Surrey days. Beryl, a keen student of the paranormal, recalled how their daughter Amanda on one occasion upstairs enquired 'Who was that lady?' when, in fact, there was nobody there.

Beryl told me too about a door which refused to stay closed.

'The door links the inner hall and the back hall. Time and again I would close it quite securely, move only a few paces and it would automatically open . . . very odd. I've also felt a cold spot on the stairs, and upstairs on a number of occasions bedroom doors have opened and closed for no apparent reason and without any logical explanation.'

Beryl then showed me the Prince's bedroom at the front of the house, and confessed: 'Here in the bathroom I have felt more than vibes, I've felt someone physically touching me, not nastily, but certainly a touching sensation. If Tredethy is haunted, then they are friendly spirits.'

I can endorse that: as a visitor to Tredethy at different times of the year, either for lunch or dinner in the evening, the same peaceful

PEACEFUL ATMOSPHERE ... Beryl Graham, left, talks to Rebecca Pickford and Michael Williams in the Prince's bedroom at Tredethy.

STAIRWAY TO THE PAST ... Rebecca Pickford of BBC Radio Cornwall, right, interviews Beryl Graham at Tredethy.

atmosphere reigns.

Perhaps the butler and the lady so loved the place they are reluctant to leave it – and who can blame them?

It is an interesting coincidence that I had a curious experience not far from Tredethy. One afternoon in November 1984 I was driving along the Bodmin to Camelford road when I saw a cyclist coming in the opposite direction from Camelford. There was nothing vague or misty about him, and I wasn't day dreaming – actually I was reflecting on the fact that the day had gone well in terms of book business – there was not a Supernatural thought in my head. Suddenly I realized he, the cyclist, was no longer ahead and yet I was convinced we had not passed one another. The picture of the man and his cycle had been so vivid that I turned the car round and drove for nearly a mile back down that road, but there was no sign of him and I am practically certain that, in the time scale, he could not have reached the next side turning ahead of me in the car. Driving back to St Teath two things stood out in my mind. First, the road had been empty; there was no other traffic involved – no question of vision being obscured for a few seconds. Secondly, on reflection the man, his clothing and his machine all somehow suggested a style of forty or even fifty years ago.

PSYCHOMETRY

BACK in the 1840s an American scientist, Professor Buchanan invented the word 'psychometry'.

A certain Bishop Polk told the professor he could identify brass in darkness by simply touching it with his fingers and the Bishop had a second method of identification: brass produced an extremely unpleasant taste in his mouth. Buchanan tested the Bishop and found all this to be perfectly true. Furthermore he discovered some of his students had the ability to identify certain objects even when wrapped in brown paper. What really baffled the professor was that some sensitives could hold a sealed letter and describe the man or woman who had written it!

It was in my first year in North Cornwall that I encountered psychometry for the first time. I made an appointment with Betty Lukey, then living at Withiel: my first experience of meeting a clairvoyant. Betty Lukey was holding my watch in her hands, using it as the means of uncovering the past and probing the future. A quarter of a century later, I can recall the astonishing accuracy of her findings – and I am certain that what she knew about me would scarcely have covered a postcard. She predicted that in the next few years I would marry a lady who had already worn a wedding ring. She further forecast that though I would be working in the hotel business for some years, my real future lay in publishing and writing. All of which came true. She did though baffle me by saying I would be involved in radio and television, and that I would be happier in the former. At that stage I thought this part of her forecasting was badly off course – nobody had ever suggested either medium.

Within a year I did my first radio broadcast, and within a few years

I was interviewed by Colin Wilson for the first colour television programme in Cornwall and thereafter made a number of TV appearances over the years although always aware of the fact that I am much happier with radio. Indeed I have now taken part in several radio series and made more than fifty broadcasts. So much for my scepticism.

Betty Lukey made one other curious prediction. 'You'll be associated with Daphne du Maurier in some significant way.' This, of course, was out of the question. I had met Dame Daphne but she was an internationally famous novelist; I was merely an aspiring author and cottage publisher.

Astonishingly, in 1973 when Bossiney was still only a part-time publisher, we launched a book called *My Cornwall*, with the opening chapter contributed by Daphne du Maurier, and another coming from her sister Angela – the only time in publishing history when the two sisters appeared inside the same book. Then, incredibly, more than twenty years later Sonia and I published a book entitled *Daphne du Maurier Country* and with Tamsin Thomas of BBC Radio Cornwall put together a radio series of the same name. Moreover on the day Dame Daphne died I was invited to appear on local and national radio and television: all uncannily confirming Betty Lukey's predictions of nearly a quarter of a century ago.

In the years I knew Betty Lukey two things stood out: her ability to tune in to complete strangers and her capacity to pick up vibrations – sometimes I wondered if she were a mind reader who didn't know it. Sadly though she seemed totally unable to see for herself, a very bad motor crash being just one example.

Possibly psychometry is a mixed form, including elements of clairvoyance and telepathy. On a number of occasions I have experimented as the psychometrist, and have often been surprised by the amount of detailed information that has come from a ring or a watch belonging to the person concerned. On the occasions when only scraps of information came, I have come to the view that either the owner and the object have not had a long and close relationship – or the owner, deep down, was cynical or attempting to hide some fact or facts.

FAMOUS AUTHOR … Dame Daphne du Maurier whose link with Michael Williams, foretold by psychometrist Betty Lukey, came uncannily true.

43

NORTH CORNWALL EXPERIENCES

A HIGH percentage of people seem to go through life without a Supernatural experience of any kind – I say seem because many of us believe many people see ghosts without being aware of the fact. The ghosts are so life-like that they are simply not identified. Other people have a single experience – as if they were in the right place at the right time, just once. Other people, seemingly a minority, keep having paranormal experiences throughout their lives.

One such man is David Waddon-Martyn who lives at The Old Millfloor, Tarbarwith, near Tintagel. Here are some of his experiences, all appearing in book form for the first time:

'It was in 1970 and I went down to Boscastle Harbour during a late afternoon in November with the purpose of doing some bass fishing beyond where the boats are moored. I took out all my fishing gear and proceeded along the harbour wall. It was an uninviting cloudy evening with a big sea roaring – good for bass – and a large swell entering the harbour. It was very windy and some cottage and street lights were already on, and I admired the shimmering reflections of the lights on the moving waters.

'As I went down the harbour wall towards where the fishing boats are moored I observed a figure of a man on his own standing past the boats at the top of hewn steps in the rock. My first impressions were that this fellow was one of the last of the holiday visitors in Boscastle and was just out for a walk, admiring the scenery of the village and inner harbour with the lights on, just as I had done. However, as I approached nearer and started to the corner of the harbour wall in preparation to ascend the steps, I observed that this man was in actual fact not looking at the harbour nor the general scene, but was staring at me, and my progress along the wall from the car.

'I knew then this man was not of this place as I saw his stare and his glazed eyes looking at me. They were distant eyes, as if thinking of the past. He was dressed in fawn type trousers of heavy twill, and three quarter length lambswool coat and a deerstalker tweed hat. He was standing with a stick in his hand, not in a support position. This man's stare changed to a more acute angle as I was then looking up at him. He then took a pace back, turned round and just 'melted away'. He disappeared – and fearful that he may have moved faster and gone over the rocks into the water, I quickly searched the whole area in question, and the sea. He was nowhere to be found.

'I then thought this was stupid of me as he would have had to travel a terrific distance on the rock area just above the steps and couldn't have achieved this in so short a time. I am convinced this was a sighting of the Supernatural, as later in the night after the fishing was over and I had driven back to Trenale Lane, Tintagel, had a late supper and retired to the sitting room, I lay down on the settee to read the newspaper – I dropped off to sleep on the sofa, the lights still on in the room, and suddenly woke up and saw the very same man now dressed in the very same clothes, standing by the sitting room door. This was definitely not a dream. However, this figure was only glimpsed briefly by the door, and after I was completely convinced he just faded away again.

'In 1969 my father died of cancer in the Exeter Hospital. The cremation service was at the Parish Church of Heavitree, the family were gathered outside, and after the coffin was removed from the hearse and put on a trolley for transport to the parish church, I observed a man – white hair and moustache – dressed in a suit – standing away from us all and appearing if he was attending the funeral. He was absolutely identical to the fellow I had seen in Boscastle and Tintagel in 1968. My father died on January 20 1969. Was this a warning to me?

'All I can say is this man whom I saw standing outside the parish church never was seen inside the church for the service, but I saw him outside before the service started. Then I cast it out of my

HARBOUR HAUNTS ... Boscastle harbour where the strange figure was seen.

mind as my thoughts were on my father. I have never seen this man since.

'Ever since the earlier Tonacombe experience – mentioned in your first book on the Supernatural – when I saw the same woman in 1943 and later in 1963 as you recorded, I have been constantly aware that I am never alone, even though my wife, daughter and son are not in the area at all. I still feel this way now – I feel it at Tonacombe and Millfloor. Very often I am aware that someone I have known in the past is around and amongst us as I smell the same pipe tobacco night and day, inside and outside the house, and sometimes at Tonacombe too. I also believe we are constantly in the care and possible protection of past loved ones who love to be in our midst.

'At Millfloor both Jamie and I in the early 1970s heard on one occasion a long and hard knock on the front door about five am and knocks on the sitting room window in the evening just before the earlier noise. There is a brass knocker on the front door, but this was not used. Possibly the knock was on another door when Millfloor was a very small cottage, going back to the 1300s. We have photos of it before Mr George Walker enlarged it.

'I will just mention another experience in 1978 at Millfloor. I was off work recuperating at Millfloor after a spell in Freedom Fields Hospital, Plymouth with internal problems. I get very bored if I do nothing even though I was meant to be taking things easy. I felt that the garden in this summer could not look after itself so I had to slash a lot of growth on the bank by the house next to the main path. An elderly woman, shortish in stature, appeared on the paved area by the house where the tea tables were and wanted just a cup of tea. She sat with her back to me. Janice served her. When it was time for her to go she had insufficient money for the bill and wrote an IOU on a small photograph of a 'peculiar' nondescript sign. I have never seen one like it.

'On this photo she wrote "IOU a penny". She got up and just vanished. I could have seen her, but I didn't, but heard the iron gate by the main path entrance open and shut as if a person was going off the premises. I looked over the wall where I expected to see this person, but no-one was there . . . no one was walking in the vicinity up or down the road. Janice was a bit surprised and thought this woman was strange. She was not a tourist and wore a long black skirt and cardigan. All I can say is that I witnessed this person seated at the tea table; but she just vanished and we didn't see her go.'

HALLOWE'EN HARVEST

IT WAS Rebecca Pickford who suggested I should take part in a ghost phone-in with Tamsin Thomas at the Truro studios of BBC Radio Cornwall on Hallowe'en morning 1990 – a very worthwhile exercise it was, with factual accounts coming in from places scattered over Cornwall.

The following are extracts from that programme.

An early call was phoned in from Sennen by Trevor Lawrence.

Tamsin Thomas: 'A benevolent spirit is abroad in Sennen. Is that right, Trev?'

Trevor Lawrence: 'Well, it used to be. Up until the middle of the last century the villagers were occasionally visited by a strange dark cloud of dense mist which used to loom up over the horizon heading in towards the cove. It would hover over the rocks for a while, and as the day went on the cloud would move right out across the entrance to Sennen Cove. As night fell showers of sparks would shoot out from the cloud, and strange hooting noises would accompany the sparks; so much so that the villagers in the cove actually called the cloud the hooter of Sennen or the hooper of Sennen. We believe that it contains some form of guardian spirit to forewarn of severe weather conditions approaching, and when the hooter appeared across Sennen Cove no fisherman would ever dare put to sea.

'At some time during the middle of last century there was a pretty cantankerous fisherman living down in the cove, and he thought that this was nothing but an old wives tale. 'Well, if I wanted to go to sea nothing would stand in my way!' He bragged about this so much that in the end it seemed that he had to put it to the test.

When the hooter appeared on the next occasion the fisherman took his son with him and the son stood in the bows of the boat and they borrowed a threshing flail from one of the local farmers, and this one actually threshed his way out through that strange cloud formation. From that day to this the hooter of Sennen has never returned back to the cove to warn fishermen of foul weather conditions approaching.'

Tamsin Thomas: 'But it was obviously taken very seriously when it was there.'

Trevor Lawrence: 'Oh yes, and the strange thing is that the fisherman and his son never returned either, it is said that if anyone is out walking along the coastal footpath between Land's End and Sennen Cove and if the wind is blowing in the right direction and the weather is on the turn for the worst, then you can still hear the fisherman and his son scrambling back up over the rocks to get back to their families back in Sennen and crying out for help.'

Tamsin Thomas: 'That really puts a shiver down your spine, doesn't it, because that's a very dramatic part of coastline isn't it, from Sennen to Land's End? It's very atmospheric too. Michael have you heard about this?'

Michael Williams: 'No, it's a completely new story to me. Absolutely fascinating because the thing we call time is like a film and it may get tangled or twisted and, as a result, we pick up fragments of other times, and that could account for people hearing voices from another time, another situation.'

Next on the line was Sue Desmond from Camborne.

Tamsin Thomas: 'You had a visit from your dead dog?'

Sue Desmond: 'Yes, I did. This experience happened to me about six months ago. We had a dog which was called Dan, and Dan met an untimely death and in a short period of time we replaced him with another dog called Ben. One evening I was in bed and I had actually gone to sleep and something awoke me. I looked by the door in the bedroom and there was our dog Ben, and I thought "Gosh, what's he doing in the bedroom," because he was rather a mischevious puppy and we'd had to lock him in the kitchen and bolt the door, and I thought "Good grief, my husband must have left the kitchen door open and he's got out. He's in the bedroom with us!" So he was standing by the door, and he was absolutely

THE HOOTER OF SENNEN … The guardian spirit which a foolish fisher-man dared to challenge.

SEA SPIRIT ... Sennen Cove in winter.

solid in shape. It was no sort of ghostly shadow and he was actually there; so I followed him up the corridor into the lounge and suddenly I lost him. We've got quite a large lounge, and we hunted around the lounge and I couldn't find him, and went to the kitchen door. The door was still bolted! It obviously wasn't Ben our new dog, it was Dan our old dog who had come back to visit us, and there's nothing I could explain: the door was locked. There was no other means of escape and it *was* our old dog Dan.'

Tamsin Thomas: 'Was it a friendly visit? Or did something happen afterwards that you thought perhaps he was warning you about?'

Sue Desmond: 'No, nothing happened after, and there's no way I can explain it. But it really unsettled me and I've just got nothing to explain it at all.'

Tamsin Thomas: 'That's an interesting one.'

Michael Williams: 'Very interesting indeed. I don't think it should disturb you, Sue. My view is that the numerous occurrences of ghostly animals suggest that animals go on. That they too go on for a further life. It's reasonable to assume that if we see ghosts of people that would suggest death is not the end, and it must be very consoling to many animal lovers – and I speak as someone who has recently lost a dear young cat – that stories such as yours really suggest that they have not died in the final sense, but they have progressed onto something else.'

Sue Desmond: 'He was definitely solid. I actually thought it was our new dog. There was nothing ghostly about him. But he ignored me; he was just sort of doing his own thing, and it was just very, very eerie when I realised it wasn't the new dog.'

Tamsin Thomas: 'It was interesting that he should have taken such a solid form. Anything that is thought of as ghostly has a shimmering apparition-like appearance attached to it, but clearly that is not always the case.'

Sue Desmond: 'He didn't walk through walls or doors, he was, as I say, solid. I thought it was the other dog.'

Tamsin Thomas: 'That doesn't surprise you Michael?'

Michael Williams: 'No, it doesn't because you're right to touch on this point of the appearance. People and animals, they can be so solid in these sightings, that people are only aware of the fact that they are ghosts, and not real when something unusual happens – such as an animal or person disappears, or goes through a solid wall. It's only when something like that happens that the realisation comes home, that this was a ghost, not a real person or animal.'

Next came an extraordinary story from Shirley Stone.

Tamsin Thomas: 'I think you've had a few experiences, but one in particular involved your son.'

Shirley Stone: 'That's right.'

Tamsin Thomas: 'Tell us about it.'

Shirley Stone: 'A few years ago, I'd gone to bed, and I was dreaming, and I dreamt of a place called Tywardreath. I don't know whether you know it at all, close to Par.'

Tamsin Thomas: 'Yes, very close to home.'

Shirley Stone: 'Straight above the hill where the roads fork off, it was terrible weather, and the roads were literally shining wet . . . rain, and there was thunder and lightning; and in the middle of this road there was a little man on a ladder climbing up into the sky. And I was so worried, I thought my goodness that little man could get struck down with lightning. Anyway, that was the dream. Next morning we were down having breakfast and my youngest son said "Wasn't it terrible weather last night mum.?" Well, I'd forgotten the dream, but I said "Was it?" and he said "Yes, it was thunder and lightning, and I got out of bed to watch it through my window." After him saying that things started clicking in my mind. "There was this little man on a ladder, and he said "Go back to bed, Kenny".' I ducked down under the window, and this little man said "I can see you Kenny, go back to bed!" Well what do you make of that.'

Michael Williams: 'I'm speechless. Here we have a sharing of a dream experience and presumably the boy not dreaming, but sharing a genuine Supernatural experience. And that must be something very rare: a Supernatural experience *and* an identical dream, and, of course, the fact that it's mother and son makes it even more interesting.'

Tamsin Thomas: 'There is a very close bond isn't there, between mother and son. This may have something to do with it.'

Michael Williams: 'Yes, but it's a baffling account, absolutely fascinating and I've heard nothing like it before in twenty five years of investigating the Supernatural.'

Tamsin Thomas: 'Well, St Austell seems to be a hotbed of interest today because we are now joined by Diane Waters from St Austell.'

Diane Waters: 'We've lived here about three years and the first winter we were here we sat down, all cosy, and we kept getting these absolutely beautiful smells, it wasn't perfume, not the made perfume, it was actually flowers we could smell. Sweet peas and

54

THOUGHTFUL PAUSE … Tamsin Thomas, who chaired the ghost phone-in looks across Dozmary Pool on Bodmin Moor from the saddle of her horse.

roses and smells like chrysanthemum – they have a different sort of smell, and we had this for ages. We thought perhaps it was the wood we were burning on the fire. We lived with it for a while, and then a friend came down to see me, and we were sat there, and she said "Where have you got your sweet peas?" "I haven't got any". "But I can smell sweet peas." It lasted for a second or two; then it was gone. This was the sort of thing, but now, to our horror, we have upstairs the most disgusting smell that comes and goes. It seems to come from the beams. We have beams in the ceiling, and they have big holes as though nails have been knocked in, and the smell seems to come from there. Sometimes it's in the air, and sometimes it's not there at all.'

Michael Williams: 'Ghostly smells do occur. They are fewer than ghostly sightings. If this lady is really worried about the unpleasant smell from the beams and it is upsetting I would suggest that she consults a clergyman as there are some members of the clergy who are equipped and trained to perform a service of blessing. That could almost certainly remove any unpleasant smell.'

Tamsin Thomas: 'Have you looked Diane, to see if there's anything unpleasant in the loft?'

Diane Waters: 'Yes, we can't really get too much in the loft; it's only a cottage with a very narrow loft, but it was all done new three years ago. The original beams were used; they were tidied up and all the woodworm killed off etc., but this smell only lasts a while, any of the smells really, the nice smells, sort of appear and go. They sort of waft under your nose then disappear. I have an old cat, wouldn't she be upset if there was something not very nice? I was always given the impression that anything like that an animal would object to.'

Michael Williams: 'Cats are amongst the most psychic animals, and I think if it were anything really unpleasant your cat would react strangely in some way.'

Diane Waters: 'Yes, I thought that.'

Tamsin Thomas: 'I think it needs further investigation, perhaps amongst the beams or in the loft. Let us know what you find.'

Tamsin Thomas: 'Sally Anne rang in from Helston. Now in her 70s, but when she was younger she used to meet this man on the stairs of her old farmhouse. He wore a long frock coat and a short pork pie hat. She got so used to him she'd dodge him going up the stairs and her great aunt used to say goodnight to him, but now the farmhouse has been made into four flats, and she doesn't know what's happened to him. Is it that when houses change perhaps they go?'

Michael Williams: 'Sometimes, not always. This is rather strange because I've known two instances in Cornwall of where staircases have been altered and ghosts have been seen walking at the original levels; in other words they are taking no account of the later developments in the change of the building. But who knows, this man might have been a restless spirit, and somehow the transformation of the building has settled his problems, because some people believe that ghosts are spirits who are reluctant to leave a place where they lived or worked, a place where they had special affection. Maybe that's the case.'

Tamsin Thomas: 'Or could he still be there, but perhaps in an area of the house where people no longer go because of the alterations?'

Michael Williams: 'Yes, that's quite possible.'

Tamsin Thomas: 'Back to the calls, we are now going to Cathy Gilbert of St Austell. I understand that you were visited by your dead father?'

Cathy Gilbert: 'Yes that's right, he died the previous afternoon, and I'd gone to bed that night and I was lying there and was obviously very upset and I thought I'm not going to go to sleep and all of a sudden he appeared: not all of him, just his face and head, and he said to me "Cathy" and I said "Yes, dad". He said "It's nice here, it's all right, and I'm free from pain." and that was it. He just went again. I didn't grieve for him after that. I knew he was somewhere better than we could be.'

Tamsin Thomas: 'How interesting, now I've heard of this happening before, a friend of mine reckoned her father came to her after dying. Is this something, Michael, that tends to happen perhaps with families that are close?'

Michael Williams: 'Yes, it does, and I hope it reassures Sue who was disturbed about her dog appearing. I think the dog was putting over the message which father was putting over in this case.'

Tamsin Thomas: 'Cathy, were you upset by it? Or were you reassured by it?'

Cathy Gilbert: 'I was reassured. Although I was unhappy at the funeral, I didn't grieve because I knew that he was much better where he was. He'd been in such a lot of pain before he died. And the other thing was I always hoped – I lived 200 miles away from him – and I hoped that when the time came I'd know. I had a funny sort of feeling come over me, and went to phone the hospital and they said "I'm sorry, your father died a few minutes ago." It was if he was telling me he was going before he actually died.'

Tamsin Thomas: 'It's an extraordinary sense, a bond that families can build up.'

Cathy Gilbert: 'That's right, I was so far away and I just felt that sudden feeling of loss. I've never grieved for him, I'm happy that he's where he is.'

Tamsin Thomas: 'Yes, that because he's been able to tell you.'

Cathy Gilbert: 'Yes, that's right, it didn't frighten me or bother me when he appeared. It was almost like a relief.'

Michael Williams: 'That's very good, Tamsin, isn't it? Because so often people think that ghosts are bad things, and say they're doing no good at all. Here is a ghostly appearance reassuring the person. That's excellent news.'

Brenda Haynes of Truro recalled a war time experience.

Brenda Haynes: 'When my brother was in the war he was torpedoed on the *Inglesfield*. He was called Albert, and that night my mother had a dream – she was holding him up. We knew nothing, the Admiralty wouldn't tell you anything. But in the paper the next morning was the *Inglesfield* had gone down with all hands. But mother said "I held him up last night in the cold water, I felt it!" We didn't hear until about three months that my brother was safe. I don't know whether other people experience these things.'

Tamsin Thomas: 'I think that is the case, isn't it Michael?'

Michael Williams: 'Yes, it is. Telepathy really is communication between one mind and another without the use of speech, or any of the normal conscious channels, and I'm sure that's what your mother and son experienced.'

Brenda Haynes: 'She said she held him up in the water. She told us that the next morning! "No, I held him up," she said. "I was in the water with him last night." We didn't hear anything for three months; only the headlines in the paper.'

Finally came a call from Anne with a Somerset story.

Tamsin Thomas: 'Tell me about your story.'

Anne: 'It was several years ago, my husband and I were coming home from the Severn Valley Railway, and we decided to pop into Glastonbury Abbey. It was fairly late and we couldn't take one of those tapes with us to tell us about the Abbey, so we just went around for a walk. At the time we had our dog with us. We walked around the Abbey and my husband said "Let's go up towards the high altar to have a close look at that." We went up towards the high altar, and all of a sudden my dog started growling and I thought: "What are you doing? Stop growling." But he wouldn't stop and we went a bit further towards the high altar, and he literally stopped dead and tried to go backwards, and he wouldn't stop growling, so we thought we'd better take him away just in case he's not happy. And we walked away, but I thought "Well, there must have been something there." So we took him back again, but he did exactly the same thing again. Now we don't know why he did it or what was there. We didn't see anything, but he *knew* there was somebody there.'

Tamsin Thomas: 'Goes back to what we were saying about dogs again doesn't it, Michael, and their intuition?'

Michael Williams: 'Yes, very interesting that here is another dog case, and I've certainly had two very vivid Supernatural experiences with dogs.'

A SPECIAL SENSE … '*Cats are among the most psychic animals* …'

Tamsin Thomas: 'It's obvious that dogs tune into these things quicker than humans.'

Michael Williams: 'I think that's so, and Glastonbury has a very haunted reputation.'

Anne: 'Yes, they reckon that King Arthur is buried there, I wouldn't have thought that he'd been buried under the high altar, but whatever it was the dog sensed it.'

Michael Williams: 'I don't think it necessarily had anything to do with Arthur at all. A member of the Ghost Club some years ago thought he was seeing a group of religious people touring the area, and he thought they were going to see some gathering in a part of the Abbey and followed them. Then when he got there the place was empty. Not a soul to be seen. So it's that type of place. I don't say it happens every day but, as I was saying earlier, time is like a film and when it gets tangled or twisted we pick up fragments of other times, and I think your dog picked up another time.'

WHAT IS LUCK?

'HAS he luck?' asked Napoleon.

An old English proverb says it is better to be born lucky than rich. If a black cat crosses the path of a Romany, he puts a wish on it.

What is luck?

In the *Collins English Dictionary*, I came across these two concise definitions: '1. 'Events that are beyond control and seem subject to chance; fortunate. 2. Success or good fortune.'

Good as they are, these definitions somehow fall short of capturing the fullness of the word. Luck is a mysterious something – like a pot of gold at the end of the rainbow.

In the several years that I was Acora's publisher and ghost writer, both he and his wife Jeannette stressed the importance of the old Romany philosophy: 'Think lucky and you'll be lucky.' Frankly this isn't merely wishful thinking. Highly intelligent students of human behaviour firmly believe feelings are of paramount importance: if we *feel* lucky, the odds are we'll attract good luck.

Could it be that imagination is a key factor in luck – that we act upon hunches and 'inspirations?' If we're negative, we are likely to attract defeat and disappointment. In contrast, if we are positive, we could be attracting success and a sense of fulfilment. If we picture ourselves happy and successful, then we could be opening the door to that very condition. By improving our mental photography we could be taking the first decisive steps towards our goal – and ambition.

Acora, a gifted clairvoyant, believes certain things bring good luck. I never knew him to do a radio or television interview without wearing something red – red being the traditional luck colour for his Scorpio sign.

Luck exists. I have no doubt about that.

Of course I am superstitious. There is always a horseshoe in my office. The theory of the lucky charm is that we concentrate our thoughts on the charm – thus creating a psychic force against any ill luck and, at the same time, producing a focus of psychic influence which attracts good luck.

Generally believed to be a bringer of good luck, and used as a protective amulet, the horseshoe has ancient connections with the mystic powers of fire and iron. The traditional pattern is to position the horseshoe to the front door – Admiral Lord Nelson nailed one to the mainmast of *HMS Victory*. The important thing is ensure that the points of the shoe are uppermost – otherwise good luck will drain away! In the old days horses were regarded as particularly vulnerable to witchcraft and ill-wishing.

Sportsmen are often notoriously superstitious, and Helston-born boxer Bob Fitzsimmons was such a character. The only Briton to win the world heavyweight crown, and the first man to hold three world titles at three different weights, Bob Fitzsimmons always kept a horseshoe nailed up at his training camp for good luck. Fitzsimmons, sometimes known as 'The Fistic Freak,' was credited with inventing that colourful defiant sporting phrase: 'the bigger they come, the harder they fall.'

Though thirteen is regarded by many people as an unlucky number – there were thirteen at the Last Supper – I have often found this number works well; so much so that I now have a habit of making important engagements for the thirteenth day of the month, especially if the thirteenth falls on a Friday! The Americans cannot be all that superstitious because the Seal of the President of the United States incorporates eight groups of thirteen stars – representing the original thirteen states.

Undoubtedly many people believe certain numbers work well for them. Traditionally we Aquarians favour four which represents the four elements: fire, air, earth and water. Seven is also rated a very powerful number – some say the most mysterious of all, due to the seven planets. The ancient Greeks and Romans regarded seven as the symbol of good fortune. Even as a boy, for some reason I cannot

GIPSY LORE ... Acora recalls that there is an old Romany tradition that a horse brings a traveller luck.

recall, 47 was my lucky number and curiously the only match-winning innings I ever played at cricket was in a game at Bristol where I had the luck and confidence to score 47 not out.

In cricket it generally appears that the confident players do best and cricket *does* reflect society and Life itself. Arnold Bennett in his volume *Mental Efficiency* touched on the subject of success:

'How comes it that men without any other talent possess a mysterious and indefinable talent to succeed? Well, it seems to me that such men always display certain characteristics, and the chief of these characteristics is the continual, insatiable wish to succeed. We others are not so preoccupied. We dream of success at intervals, but we have not the passion for success . . .'

A few years ago my club, the Cornish Crusaders, were playing Gloucestershire 2nd XI in Cornwall and the cricket of the young visiting professionals was very confident, positive and purposeful. I remarked on this to John Shepherd, the Gloucestershire county coach, and he replied: 'I always want our boys to go out on to the field *expecting to do well*.' There was nothing arrogant in his tone. The expectation was based on sound technique and a positive mental approach.

Barney Camfield in an earlier Bossiney title *Healing, Harmony & Health* dealt very specifically with ambition:

'To summarise: First of all you will find that it is completely useless to attempt to succeed at anything at all if you consciously allow thoughts of failure or the sense of depression to remain in your mind. Think of something positive and cheerful – BE OPTIMISTIC! – and you will cancel the wrong thoughts out.

'Secondly: don't try too hard for success; just confidently hope and expect it to arrive. If you try and force things you are liable to make mistakes and be clumsy over it – just as you were when you consciously tried to swing the pendulum. The same law is in force, you see; if you believe that the job in hand is hard, then your sub-conscious will see that you do the wrong things, in order to make it hard! You can safely leave it to your sub-conscious mind to prompt you and give you ideas. You will know when to make a move and when to sit tight and do nothing.

'Thirdly: keep on thinking of yourself as you wish to be – completely ignoring the failures you had in the past.

'Fourthly: make sure of your goal before you allow your sub-conscious to guide you on your way. Ask yourself quite honestly what it is you want –

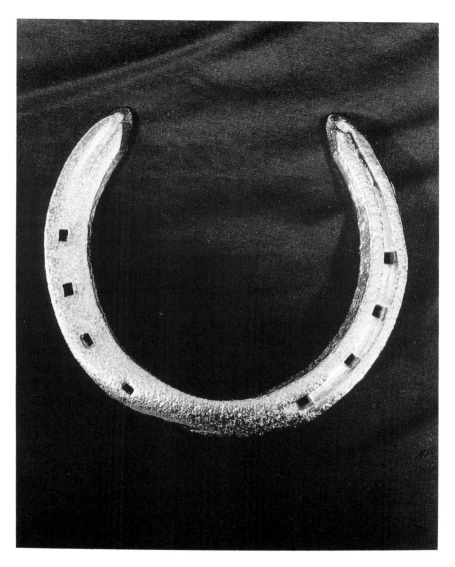

POPULAR SYMBOL ... The horseshoe, traditional bringer of good luck, is to be found at cottage doors and pub entrances all over Cornwall – and much further afield. But the points of the shoe must always point upwards or all that good luck will just fall out!

and why you want it! Do you want to be wealthy? Why? Because being wealthy you think that you will then be happy? Do you want to be famous – as a musician or an athlete? Why? Because it'll make you happy? That's the real goal – HAPPINESS! That's what you are really after!'

Visualization is a vast subject. Have we perhaps strayed from luck? But then that's the *Supernatural:* many facets.

What about Goethe? As a young man he discovered when out for a walk he sometimes felt the desire to see his ladylove – whoever she was at the time – and before long she would appear, somehow moved to come to *this spot*. Goethe had the ability to visualize sharply. If he shut his eyes and imagined a rose, then he would see it clearly, vividly.

Mark Twain went some steps beyond Goethe. Frequently he experienced telepathy. He became annoyed by the crossing of letters in the post and decided to do something about it: 'Now, when I get tired of waiting upon a man whom I very much wish to hear from, I sit down and *compel* him to write, whether he wants to or not; that is to say, I sit down and write him, and then tear up my letter, satisfied that my act has forced him to write to me at the same moment . . . I do not need to mail my letter . . . the writing it is the only essential thing.'

POWERFUL DRIVE ... Edward Nicolson plays a telling shot for the Crusaders – how much does confidence play a part in this country cricket match or in the world beyond the boundary?

SPIRITS GALORE AT LAUNCESTON

IN September 1986 I visited lovely Dockacre House at Launceston when helping to make a BBC Radio Cornwall series 'Ghost Hunt'. Dockacre was a destination which selected itself, for this beautiful building dating back to the first Elizabeth, the home of Lt. Col. Raymond Buckeridge and his wife Dennise, has quite a haunted reputation.

In that programme I said: 'You get the feeling of expectation as you move from room to room. The feeling that something could happen at any time, as likely to occur during the day as the night.' On three subsequent visits: the same reaction. But there is nothing threatening in the atmosphere. The 'other resident or residents' are happy – that anyway is the impression. The third step on the main staircase may seem 'colder' and different from the rest, but no menace – just that very, very cold sensation.

'On the steep slope of the hill, clinging to its side was the quaintest conceivable house – long narrow range of gables, roof and walls encased in small slate-like mail armour . . . The foundations of the houses in the street above are higher than the tops of the chimneys.'

That was how Sabine Baring-Gould described Dockacre in his novel *John Herring*, published in the late 1800s. Baring-Gould, parson, squire, author and hymn writer, lived just over the Cornwall-Devon border at Lewtrenchard, but he stayed here at Dockacre during the writing of *John Herring*. Where the garage now stands was a summer house, and it was here that the great man did most of his writing. He has given us a word picture:

'In front of the house is a narrow terrace with, at one end, a sort of summer-house, furnished with fireplace and chimney. This summer-house stood

at the edge of the terrace between the garden-gate and the house. This house was, in fact, a room of fair size, furnished with a fireplace and carved mantlepiece, that contained a quaint old painting on a panel.'

In November 1990 Raymond Buckeridge told me he had written an account of the strange happenings at his Launceston home. The following is his story.

SPIRITS GALORE

It was 'love at first sight'. No, this is not the usual love story but the story of a romance between a house and the Buckeridges who bought Dockacre House in Launceston over twenty years ago in 1968.

Little did we know that most of the problems which would have to be solved over the years would be connected with the 'spirits' that still roam the double staircase and many rooms both upstairs and down.

In a funny sort of way I think the 'spirits' quite like us and have accepted us in their house. Perhaps it is that we are not afraid of them. We accept each other as members of the family and we acknowledge the fact that we are newcomers while they have been in residence for many years, perhaps centuries.

Hanging in the dining room of our home are two pastel portraits which, it is believed, have hung there since about 1714. These portraits are of Nicholas Herle and his wife Elizabeth. Nicholas is supposed to have murdered his wife on Christmas Day 1714, although there is no evidence that he did in fact do so. It is perfectly true, however, that she did die on Christmas Day 1714 for the church burial records testify to this fact.

There are three theories concerning her death. The first is that he shot her on the third step of the left-hand staircase. The second theory is that she went mad and he locked her in a tiny upstairs room until she died of starvation. The third and more recent theory is that she died of anorexia nervosa. It may well be that Nicholas did accidentally shoot and wound Elizabeth on the staircase at some time. Perhaps she was so upset and unhappy about this that she decided to starve herself to death. Blood stains on the third step, of which there have been many reported sightings, have long since vanished with time.

A memorial in St Mary Magdalene Church, Launceston, which is behind the organ loft, states that she died on Christmas Day 1714 of 'starvation or other unlawful means'. Perhaps the words 'other unlawful means' refer to possible witchcraft. Who knows what is the correct interpretation?

Nicholas is expected sometimes to appear in the main hall, playing a merry tune on a flute which is now part of an increasing collection of walking sticks.

By tradition every owner of Dockacre House adds a personal walking stick to the collection when he or she sells the house. When we bought the house we inherited thirteen walking sticks which, again by tradition, have to be left in a sack in the attic, in a special order. It is said that if the sticks are not left in this special order, known only by the owner and passed on by word of mouth, then they will rattle all night until they have sorted themselves out into the correct order again.

I overheard someone the other day talking about 'ghosties and ghoulies and things that go bump in the night'. It reminded me of the time that something really did go bump in the night.

One midnight there was a repeated 'bump bump' in the vicinity of the main staircase. On investigation my wife, Dennise, discovered that a large picture had come off the wall, bounced down ten stairs, hit a blanket chest on the very small lower landing, turned 90 degrees and gone down four more stairs to land at the foot of the staircase, completely undamaged. The eerie thing about this incident was that not only was the frame and glass unbroken but the cord was intact and the picture hook was still in the wall.

I awoke at about 4am one Christmas Eve on hearing my wife going down the back spiral staircase which leads from our bedroom to the back hall. Her footsteps were clearly audible on the then uncarpeted staircase. On questioning her next morning, she denied even getting out of bed. Later, to my horror, on going into the drawing room I discovered that a fragile Adam style mirror had fallen off the wall and was lying undamaged on the wooden arm of a settee. The wire and nylon cord were clearly cut as if by a very sharp knife.

◀ *WHERE SPIRITS ROAM ... Dockacre House, Launceston overlooked by St Mary's Church and Launceston Castle.*

Our milkman no longer delivers our milk before dawn due to an experience he had some years ago. On walking down the drive at 5am he happened to look up at the bedroom windows, something he had never done before. To his amazement, he saw the bewigged figure of a man looking down directly at him. The milk was left on the doorstep and he scurried off looking neither to his left nor right. Since then no milkman has delivered our milk until broad daylight.

Late one evening quite recently I had contact with an unknown hand. I had been putting empty bottles into the cupboard under the left-hand staircase for later disposal. The door to this cupboard is next to a table upon which stands a brass lamp. On this particular occasion I had switched on neither hall nor cupboard lights. Closing the cupboard door, I felt the distinct touch of a hand on my shoulder. I jerked my head round to see who was there but there was no one. Or was there?!

That incident reminds me of the visit, soon afterwards, of a ghost researcher. As we were about to ascend the main staircase to tour the house he moved in front of the table which is very near the cupboard in question. It also happens to be opposite the third step of the left-hand staircase. He stepped back and said that he felt the presence of a ghost as his neck was very stiff and the hairs were standing up on the back of his neck. Were these two incidents connected?

Our nephew John, a man of nearly forty years of age and a city banker, came to stay with us in October 1987. After watching television for a while one evening, Dennise and I went to bed leaving John to finish watching a play. The next day he told me that whilst he was watching the television our dog, Honey, kept scratching at the dining room door asking to be let in. Refusing to let her in at first but finally relenting, he went to the door, put his hand on the knob and, at that moment, the scratching on the door intensified. Opening the door John saw Honey fast asleep in her basket, some twenty feet away.

John there and then decided to go to bed but he was not to be left in peace; on dozing off he sensed the bedroom door suddenly opening. He was out of bed in a flash, and after shutting the door very securely, got back into bed. Very soon, the door inched open again. This time John shut, locked and bolted it. A peaceful, if rather sleepless, night was endured until morning.

Later that day I asked him whether he had experienced any other feelings in the house. He said that there were three things which bothered him: he had always mentally to fight his way past the third step where he would meet an icy barrier; nothing would make him enter the little overhanging room where Elizabeth Herle was supposed to have died and as for walking along the back wall of the house, this was for him forbidden territory. After much persuasion he agreed to accompany me and we walked it together. Suddenly he stopped: 'Another icy barrier', he said. Not knowing the relationships of the parts of the house it is significant that where he stopped was exactly opposite the third step, the room overhanging the staircase and in direct line with the cupboard, table and lamp in the main hall!

There is really a very peaceful and happy atmosphere in the house. Dogs that have lived here with us, have never, to our knowledge, been disturbed in any way. Nothing that has happened to us has been frightening, and nothing has ever been broken or damaged. We and the spirits unseen have all lived together in peace and harmony and I hope with love and understanding for a beautiful old house.

> *'I will be correspondent to command,*
> *And do my spiriting gently'.*

William Shakespeare.

THE THIRD STEP ... Colonel Raymond Buckeridge and his wife Dennise with the sack containing the walking sticks – sitting on the staircase with the strange reputation.

THE SEA BEYOND … An entrance to Tintagel Castle.

KING ARTHUR AT TINTAGEL

IN HIS book *Ghosts of Cornwall* Peter Underwood, the President of The Ghost Club, has said: . . . *'there have been reported glimpses of the ghostly figure of the great king among these dark ruins and certainly the atmosphere is conducive to such experiences; the aura of mystery that has surrounded Tintagel for centuries has not yet disappeared.*

'That there is a strange and mystic influence hereabouts is evident from the number of people who believed that they have seen or sensed something of the past among these black cliffs and crumbling ruins where, even on the sunniest days, there is a sombre stillness, broken only by the sound of the ever-roaring sea.

'The ruined castle, once a year, is thought by some people to disappear and reappear in all its former glory, before returning to its present condition.'

Perhaps that controversial cleric Bernard Walke came to the centre of the subject when he reflected: 'I do not know what historic evidence there is for connecting Tintagel with the Holy Grail legend, but I am convinced something of spiritual import happened here.'

Having lived at nearby Bossiney for ten years, I know what Bernard Walke meant. There *is* a deep sense of something mysterious . . .

It is to Tintagel that we come for the birth of Arthur – and there are two versions. Geoffrey of Monmouth in his imagination saw this dramatic fortress on the north Cornish coastline as the birthplace for Arthur: a good choice. We must remember this Welsh Bishop, back in the twelfth century, wrote to satisfy a thirst for romance, bravery and chivalry all those years ago, and if he were able to travel on some time machine, forward into the last years of the twentieth century, he would be intrigued to find the same thirst.

Geoffrey of Monmouth's story of the birth went like this:

Uther Pendragon, king of Britain, became infatuated with Ygraine, wife of Gorlois, Duke of Cornwall, the most beautiful woman in the kingdom. The king's interest in her was such that her husband kept her virtually a prisoner at Tintagel. Infuriated, Uther descended on Cornwall. Such was his longing for the woman that Merlin the wizard prescribed a magic brew enabling him to look like the twin brother of Gorlois. Thus disguised, he had no difficulty in entering the Castle and that night he slept with Ygraine. As a result Arthur was conceived. Gorlois was defeated and killed in battle with Uther's army, and his wife, now liberated, became queen of Britain.

The second version of Arthur's birth is charged with magic and Supernatural powers. Some writers have even suggested Arthur was conceived of the gods. Again if you stand here on the cliffs at Tintagel on a stormy day, with an angry Atlantic climbing the walls of the cliffs, you can, in the eye of your imagination, picture Merlin's acceptance of the babe from the ocean.

Whichever version we accept, Merlin will always live on at Tintagel, for directly below the ruins is Merlin's Cave. Full of atmosphere and drama, this is a magical cave cutting right through to a small rocky beach on the other side of the headland. It is interesting to reflect Cornwall is often known as the Land of Merlin, and we cannot begin to understand Arthur until we know Merlin, and appreciate his influence on Arthur, the boy and the king.

Not surprisingly then Rebecca and I included Tintagel Castle ruins in our *Secret Cornwall* series for Radio Cornwall. We talked above the beach and below the great headland which thrusts out like a giant's fist into the blue-grey Atlantic.

This is a paradox of a place. Despite the fact that it's visited by thousands of people every year, it remains a mysterious place at the heart of the Arthurian enigma in Cornwall.

Some time before that broadcast I had interviewed a psycho-expansion group here in the Westcountry – members of which claim not only to have lived in Arthurian times but to have been Arthurian characters. One housewife, who nowadays lives just across the Tamar in Devon, is convinced she was Arthur in an earlier life.

Rebecca, a born news gatherer with something of Miss Marple in her make-up, was keen to interview 'Arthur', and this is what he told her:

'It was about 474 AD and we were at what is known as Drake's Island now but it was St Michael's island then, and I was moving up the Tamar and then moved into Cornwall with a band of men. It was sort of camping conditions. We were making weapons and that kind of thing. This man who I was was an extraordinarily sensitive person. He was very strong, he knew what he wanted, he was single minded. Obviously he was chosen in effect by the other tribal leaders to discover how they could get as many as they could together in order to keep the coast free of problems. Now I didn't know anything about Arthur. I haven't been tremendously interested in any of this, you know, privately, in private reading, so I was a very great 'newy' towards all this. I had no preconceived ideas. We got to the

ARTHUR'S CASTLE … The north gate at Tintagel.

valley, and I didn't even know Tintagel very well, I think I'd been there once before during the research. I have since been back, but having said that, we arrived and I remember in doing this recall, we moved up on to the island part of Tintagel, and there was a number of buildings, mostly of stone and of wood, it was a sort of monastery. As I researched I found that it was a hospice now. People came there to be cured. There was a great beautiful herb garden on that cliff, all walls round. There was a sort of crypt. This place was like a watchtower if you like.'

'What about the hard and fast evidence of this then?' asked Rebecca. 'I mean the weaponry, has it ever been found?'

'Well this is one of my ambitions: to actually find an artefact which belonged to Arthur, and I feel that somewhere in the vicinity I shall be able to find something belonging to him.'

Psycho-expansion, of course, not only goes back in time. The claim is that it is able to go forward. In a more recent interview with the lady who says she was King Arthur, I obtained from her this belief: one day, at a future date, once and for all, the reality of Arthur will be proved – and proved here in Cornwall.

BOSSINEY – AND BEYOND

IN OUR years at Bossiney we had a number of experiences in the cottage. On many occasions, we heard the sound of a door opening and footsteps climbing the stairs. The frequency was such that we accepted it all naturally. We never 'broadcast' the fact for fear of frightening any nervous guests because just occasionally we used one of the cottage bedrooms as a letting bedroom. It was only after a few years of these happenings that we learned, from an aged neighbour, how a young girl had fallen down these stairs and died as a result of her serious head injuries. We therefore assumed that, in spirit, she was returning to her former home and possibly retracing her final ascent of the narrow staircase. Our successors, the Wrightham family, heard no such footsteps, but more than once saw a ghostly monk-like figure in the dining room. Curiously in our ten years we never saw anything in the hotel itself which defied human explanation.

Undoubtedly there is a strong atmosphere about Bossiney. In March 1988 Mr H.C. Bullock wrote to me from Watford:

'After reading your book *Occult in the West* I feel I must write to you.

'In August 1986 my wife, son, daughter, grandson and myself, spent a week's holiday at Bossiney in a chalet bungalow.

'Down a stony path and a few steps was Bossiney Cove. My wife and I did not speak about it until much later in the holiday, but we both agreed that we did not like the cove. There was an atmosphere about it and we would not spend time there again although we did need to go down once more with my grandson, who was fourteen years old at that time.

'Other people seemed to enjoy the cove, walking over the fallen boulders and swimming, including my grandson, who called to me "Come and look at this cave grandad," but though I went near I had no inclination to go inside even though I am not claustrophobic. Caves and mines have no worry for me, only heights, which frighten me. My wife is quite the opposite which brings me to her experience at Bossiney.

'Looking out to sea, you will know that a cliff path goes to the right of Bossiney Cove leading round a bit of cliff face and opens up into a hollow (for want of a better description) with a waterfall. A pleasant spot, I thought, after following my son and daughter along the path.

'Wanting to show my wife this spot, the opportunity didn't arise until our last day. A wind was blowing from inland and out to sea as we cut across from the gate at the top of the sloping field down to the cliff path, missing out some of the path. Again I was following when we reached the turn round the cliff. Then my wife stopped right in front of me, turned, looked back, pointed and said "But that over there isn't Bossiney Cove."

'I knew as I looked back I should not have done so. My nerve completely went and my wife went on on her own, while I sat and waited. When she returned, unable to get down to see the waterfall, we split up, I not being able to walk back along the cliff path went across the field to the top, my wife walking back along the complete path.

'Only just now talking about your book, my wife told me that when she walked past the spot we had taken, a fear came over her, almost a panic as though a presence was around her, and she was being closely watched, which for her is unusual. Even now she can remember that terrible feeling.'

In April the same year, I heard from a painter in Santa Rosa. She told me how on a visit to Bossiney she had a sense of 'coming home, being welcomed by I don't know whom, a great sense of joy and reverence . . . I now have instant photographic recall of all the

◀ *A SOURCE OF MYSTERY ... Michael Williams at the Petrifying Well, Bossiney.*

CASCADE … St Nectan's waterfall which beckons the visitor with that power of attraction always associated with moving water.

REJUVENATING ... St Nectan's Glen which has its own healing kind of energy for those who can sense it.

places, very deeply etched in my mind but difficult to convey. There is a rejuvenating healing kind of energy emanating from the St Nectan's Glen area.'

Woods are secret places, mysterious too.

That great Liberal Lloyd George talked of 'magic and enchanted woods of Celtic antiquity,' and Wordsworth wrote '. . . there is a spirit in the woods.' Perhaps most fascinating of all was George Meredith who challenged us: 'Enter these enchanted woods, You who dare.'

As a student of the Supernatural, I am not in the least surprised that many ghosts have been located in wooded areas. This wooded glen leading up to St Nectan's waterfall is the most haunted valley in all Cornwall. This is truly a secret place. Ghostly monk figures in grey, invisible music, mocking laughter are only some of the manifestations. I have talked with more than a dozen people who have had strange experiences hereabouts – happenings which defy all rational explanation.

Charles Bayfield told me how he had seen his father in their garden down the lane by the glen, only to discover later that his father was then at Launceston twenty-one miles away! That happened more than once to Charles. In another lane nearby a resident told me how she had clearly seen a ghost cottage – a solid building that was there, and then simply wasn't there. In the same lane there were occasions when Siamese cats chased and fought with invisible enemies. If only the trees in St Nectan's Glen could talk.

Many woods generate the air of a place untrodden, an impression intensified in autumn. There is a sentence in that lovely Cornish novel *Castle Dor*, written by the then living author Dame Daphne du Maurier and a dead one Sir Arthur Quiller-Couch: 'I think that behind everybody's thoughts while he is growing there must be a forest.'

SECRET PLACES … *'Woods are secret places, mysterious too.'*

Writers seem drawn to woods, and often you find woods a recurring theme in their writing. I remember meeting Ronald Duncan shortly after the publication of his brilliant but controversial autobiography *How to make Enemies*. Ronald believed all autobiography contained a good deal of falsification for the simple reason we retain so little:

'If a man lives twenty-five thousand days how many of them can he remember? Not more than a couple of hundred at the most. But the rest were days he lived: they fell like leaves trodden underfoot.'

Trees frequently feature in our dreams. Dream interpreters say they can be a comment on our maturity or immaturity – or spiritual growth. Large dark trees can intimidate. The wish to fell a tree can be related to guilt, fear or inhibition. Trees, of course, give protection and shade, and, in our dream world, they can refer to our friends – the solid oak personifying loyal friendship.

TREES AROUND … where images crowd in and the real and unreal blend.

REFLECTIONS

I T WAS the writer Wallace Nichols who said to me: 'There's always the problem of knowing how and when to finish.' That was a conversation back in the 1960s, but I remember Wallace and his words as I approach the end of this Supernatural Search.

In my desk are the names and addresses of people all wanting to talk about their Supernatural experiences here in Cornwall. Truly life goes on: one thing leading to another – all of which reminds us that Supernatural experience is often an ongoing business and, in many instances, it is simply impossible to write the final sentence. There was one family who shifted their home on three occasions, and each time were pursued by some spirit. Confirmation that spirits travel?

At the outset I mentioned the power of the Cornish landscape. Recently somebody asked me about the most powerful places in Kernow: the best locations. Of course, different people have different responses. As some people are colour blind or dyslexic, others, in my opinion, cannot respond to atmosphere – or psychic possibility.

Then there is another category – sensitive characters who find contrasting responses to the same location. Many people experience a heightened sense of well-being on Glastonbury Tor in Somerset, but the author Colin Wilson told me: 'If I walk up the Tor with a plastic dowsing rod in my hands, it twists up and down with a strength and persistence that makes my fingers tired. My wife, who is a far better dowser than I am, found that the 'field' of

ROCKY VALLEY … where images crowd in and the real and unreal blend.

MEDIEVAL WORLD … Tintagel Castle.

the Tor made her feel sick.'

Despite that strange experience with Tex the terrier on the summit of Rough Tor, I put it high in the Cornish charts and not because it's the second highest point in all Cornwall. In the words of Bossiney colleague Elaine Beckton: 'Rough Tor has a healing quality.' Then there are the Kennack Sands down on the Lizard; Sonia and I have walked across them on many occasions – in good weather and wild – we've always found that stretch of coastline a positive tonic. Down at the other end of Cornwall Chun Castle and Quoit both come into the same league. Tamsin Thomas, author of our recently published *Mysteries in the Cornish Landscape*, was with me on the last visit. She simply said: 'What a wonderful atmosphere' and those four words said it all.

Sir Oliver Lodge, the celebrated scientist who was brave enough to become involved in psychical research, wrote in 1908:

'Take for example a haunted house . . . wherein some one room is the scene of some long past tragedy. On a psychometric hypothesis, the original tragedy has been literally photographed on its material surroundings, nay, even on the ether itself, by reason of the intensity of emotion felt by those who enacted it.'

In Cornwall there are spots where the reverse is true – as if some great *good* events have been 'photographed' on the landscape, and herein lies some of the mystery and magic of the place.

Not for nothing did C.E. Vulliamy in 1925 reflect: 'The legends and ghostly stories of Cornwall seem to grow so inevitably out of the landscape and out of the minds of the people . . .'

'The most beautiful experience we can have, is the mysterious.'

ALBERT EINSTEIN, 1931

Hear the voices of the Bard,
Who present past and future sees;
Whose ears have heard the Holy Word
That walked among the ancient trees.

WILLIAM BLAKE 1757-1827

ACKNOWLEDGEMENTS

The great majority of these accounts appear in book form for the first time, and I am indebted to people who have given me interviews on this *Supernatural Search* – special thanks also to Rebecca Pickford and Tamsin Thomas at BBC Radio Cornwall. For yet another publication the drawings of Felicity Young and the photographs of Ray Bishop bring high visual quality. Last but not least, my thanks to Linda Turner who has typed the manuscript and Angela Larcombe for her thoughtful work as Bossiney Editor.

MORE BOSSINEY BOOKS ...

GHOSTS OF CORNWALL
by Peter Underwood

Peter Underwood, President of the Ghost Club, journeys across haunted Cornwall. Photographs of haunted sites and drawings of ghostly characters all combine to prove that Cornwall is indeed a mystic land.

'Britain's top ghost-hunter ... fascinating ...' The Sunday Independent

GHOSTS OF DEVON
by Peter Underwood

Peter Underwood, President of the Ghost Club, writes of ghostly stories that saturate the county of Devon, a land full of mystery and ghostly lore and legend.

'Packed with photographs, this is a fascinating book.' Herald Express

WESTCOUNTRY HAUNTINGS
by Peter Underwood

'The Westcountry offers ... just about every kind of ghostly manifestation ...' writes Peter Underwood, President of the Ghost Club. *'... a chilling look at hauntings from Bristol to Cornwall ... many of the accounts appear for the first time.'*

David Henderson, The Cornish Guardian

E.V. THOMPSON'S WESTCOUNTRY
This is a memorable journey: combination of colour and black-and-white photography.

'Stunning photographs and fascinating facts make this an ideal book for South West tourists and residents alike – beautifully atmospheric colour shots make browsing through the pages a real delight.' Jane Leigh, Express & Echo

SUPERNATURAL INVESTIGATION
by Michael Williams

KING ARTHUR IN THE WEST
by Felicity Young & Michael Williams

GHOSTLY ENCOUNTERS
by Peter Underwood

We shall be pleased to send you our catalogue giving full details of our growing list of titles for Devon, Cornwall, Dorset, Somerset and Wiltshire and forthcoming publications. If you have difficulty in obtaining our titles, write direct to Bossiney Books, Land's End, St Teath, Bodmin, Cornwall.